THE USBORNE
SPY'S
GUIDEBOOK

Illustrated by Colin King

Original material by:
Judy Hindley, Falcon Travis, Ruth Thomson,
Heather Amery, Christopher Rawson, Anita Harper

Edited by Lesley Sims

Designed by Michèle Busby

Senior Designer: Russell Punter

How to be a spy

With this guidebook, you will enter the secret and mysterious world of spies. The book contains everything a spy needs to know, from writing coded messages to creating brilliant disguises which will fool even the cleverest enemy.

There are tips for following suspects, ideas for making a kit to take on missions, and puzzles and games to test and improve spying skills. By the end of the book, any spy will be ready to go out and uncover the enemy's secrets.

Passing messages

One of a spy's most important skills is sharing information with his fellow spies, or contacts, without the enemy noticing. He may need to pass on details of the enemy's plans, or even arrange an emergency meeting. Spies can either meet in person, known as a rendezvous*, or leave a message to be picked up later.

Using a letterbox

A 'letterbox' is a person who keeps messages for spies. This spy hides secret messages in his library books. The librarian passes them on to his contact.

A rendezvous

THIS PAINTING IS MAGNIFICENT!

An art gallery is a useful place to meet a contact. You can pretend you have come to see the paintings.

This should confuse the enemy, but have an emergency plan ready in case you are watched.

Arrange to pass a message secretly. The spies above have exchanged books with messages hidden inside.

*say *ron-day-voo*

The newspaper ploy

There are many other ways to pass a written message secretly to a contact. You could hide your message in a newspaper.

Agree to meet your contact on a park bench. Sit and read the paper for a while. When you go, leave the paper behind.

Before an enemy sneaks up, your contact picks up the paper. She reads it and leaves, taking the paper and its message with her.

Pen pals

Meet by a notice board, but don't let on that you know each other. Pretend you want to take notes and ask to borrow a pen.

Carry an identical pen, with your message hidden inside the barrel or cap. Hand this one over instead when you 'return' the pen.

The bag switch

The bag switch is similar to the pen trick. Hide messages in bags which look the same. Switch bags as you pass each other.

The borrowed map

Tell your contact to hide the message in a map. Then, stand outside a public building or tourist office, looking lost.

As she comes up, act as if she is a stranger. Ask to borrow the map. Slide the message out before giving the map back.

Changing hats

Hide messages in your hats and go separately to a café. Hang up the hats when you arrive. When you go, take each other's hats.

Leaving messages

Secret message

Sometimes a spy can pass messages without meeting anyone. Instead, he goes to a place he and his contact have agreed upon and leaves a message there. This place is called a drop. Later on, his contact can visit the drop and collect the message.

It's a good idea to have several drops, in case one is being watched by an enemy agent.

Keep each drop out of sight of the others. This makes it hard for the enemy to watch them all at once.

Walk slowly, going to the drop. Stop to look at flowers or birds so you don't arouse suspicion.

Choosing a drop

Check out the area carefully. Watch people coming and going and see what happens at different times of the day.

Approach the drop from all directions. Could a passer-by catch sight of you? How could you avoid being seen?

Find somewhere you can remain hidden from view without attracting attention while you hide the message.

The drop behind the wall is hidden by a bend in the path.

This hollow log could be a drop, but the spy would have to make sure the path was clear before using it.

Plan your route to the drop. If it looks risky, go on to the next one.

The hole in this tree trunk is a useful drop, because the tree hides spies as they leave or collect messages.

If someone comes along the path, the spy can pretend to be watching the bird.

Dangerous drops

Each of the spies shown here is about to leave a message at his drop (shown as a star). But four of them have chosen badly. They could even risk discovery. Would you have made the same mistakes?

✔ The spy can quickly check all the nearby paths, and the shrubbery hides him. If anybody walks by, he can pretend to be looking at the statue.

✔ Here, the spy has good cover and can easily check all the paths. If he has to wait for someone to pass, the pond gives a good excuse for hanging around.

✘ This path is no good – the spy can be seen from the distance in both directions. He would have to wait a long time to be alone. Someone might get suspicious.

✘ Although the hedge seems like a good place, look again. Someone could be watching the spy's every move from the upper floor of the building opposite.

✔ This is ideal. The spy can see a long way off and can hide quickly.

✔ If the spy comes in from the main path and walks halfway around the bush, he can check the whole area.

✘ The spy is well covered here – but so is anyone following him.

✘ This is no good because the spy goes from the main path to one which leads nowhere. That looks suspicious.

✔ There are good lookout points at each end of this stretch of path. The spy can see anyone coming from a long way away and the trees offer cover.

Hiding places

In this picture, there are eight places to hide a message. Keep your eyes open for possible drops the next time you're out. Good spies are always on the lookout for new hiding places.

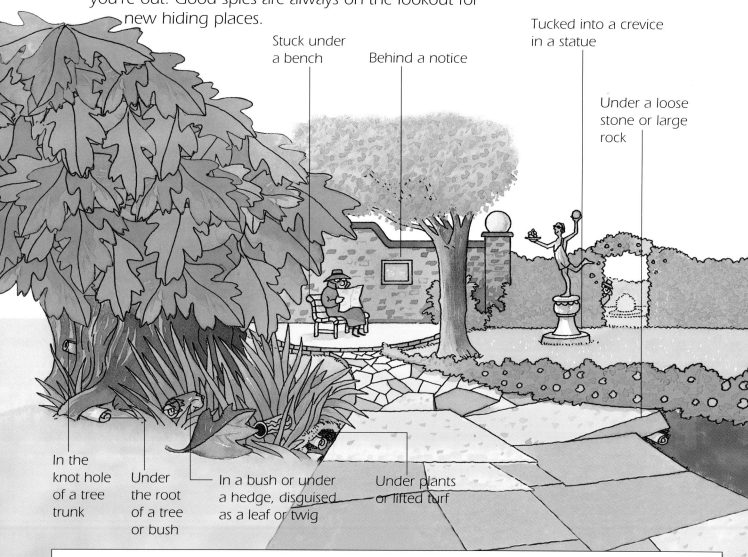

Stuck under a bench

Behind a notice

Tucked into a crevice in a statue

Under a loose stone or large rock

In the knot hole of a tree trunk

Under the root of a tree or bush

In a bush or under a hedge, disguised as a leaf or twig

Under plants or lifted turf

Disguising the message

Roll up the message tightly and tie it with thread. Your contact can use the thread to pull it out of its hiding place.

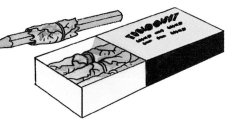

To hide it in a leaf, roll a leaf around a pencil, tie it and let it dry. Slip the leaf off the pencil and slide your message inside.

Use a screwdriver to make a hole in the cane or stick.

Smooth the inside with sandpaper.

To make the message look like a twig, hollow out a cane or large stick and hide the message inside it.

Signposts

To tell a contact which drop you used, leave a sign at a second spot, or signpost. Give the signs names and note them in a book. Here are some ideas for signs.

Leaf signs

Tear off some leaf to lengthen the stalk.

Back view

SFB: *stalk through leaf from front to back* – There's a message at drop 1.

SBF: *stalk through leaf from back to front* – Look for a message at drop 2.

TS: *twig through stalk* – Urgent! Collect message at drop 3.

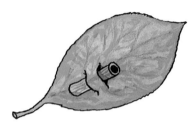

TBL: *twig through back of leaf* – Avoid all drops today. Try again tomorrow.

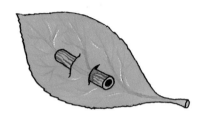

TFL: *twig through front of leaf* – Leave now. Our cover is blown.

Using a signpost

Pretend to be fiddling with a leaf. (It is one you have already marked in secret.)

Wander past a plant and casually drop the leaf into the plant pot.

The plant pot is a signpost. The leaf will tell your contact which drop to visit.

Later, you can check to see if it has been picked up by your contact . . .

. . . or if she has replaced it with a new signal, giving you a reply.

Collect any signal you find, so that your contact knows you have seen it.

Signpost tactics

These spies are checking different signpost signals (see below). Always behave casually while waiting to use a signpost.

With practice, you will be able to use one even when you are being watched. Learn to memorize the signals at a glance.

If you have to kneel down to leave or pick up a signal, think of a good reason for doing it. You could pretend to pull up your socks.

Pretend to tie a shoelace as you check a signal.

Knots in the string are a signal. Collect.

Pretend to trail your hand along the railing and slip off the code string.

This chalk mark is a signal. Rub it out.

Always remove a signal before collecting a message from a drop. Then your contact knows the message has been taken, without returning to the drop to check.

Signpost signals

These codes are made up of dots and dashes written on stones, or long and short knots tied in pieces of string.

Use whichever code is easiest to hide at your signpost. Keep a secret note of all of the codes in a book.

Write L for a long knot and S for a short knot.

1. Message at drop 1

2. Message at drop 2

3. Avoid drops – plan 1

4. Message not found

To make a short knot, loop the string like this and pull it tight.

For a long knot, loop the string like this and pull tight.

Are you being watched?

However careful you are, someone may see you going to a drop. What can you do if you think you're being watched?

The general rule is NEVER look directly at the suspect. Pretend that you're not interested in him or that you haven't even seen him.

But if he is obviously watching you, make it clear you've noticed him. With his cover blown, he will probably disappear.

Is the suspect an enemy spy?

To check out a suspect, choose a false drop away from the others which you can watch secretly.

Get the suspect to follow you. Look as suspicious as you can, but don't give yourself away.

When he's following you, lead the suspect to the false drop. You don't have to take the shortest route.

At the drop, be careful not to let the suspect see whether you are collecting or delivering a message.

When the suspect checks the drop, it will be empty. He'll think that you have just collected a message.

You can go. The suspect will now watch the false drop for the next delivery, leaving the real ones alone.

Hidden messages

If you need to give your contacts the route to your drops, make an invisible map using the trick shown here. Only someone who knows the secret can make it appear. These pages also show you how to write invisible letters.

1. Draw a pencil map of the area around your drops. Wet it with cold water and lay it on newspaper.

2. Put a sheet of paper on top. Add the route and drops in pencil. Press hard. Then remove the top sheet.

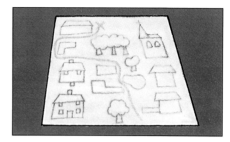

3. As the map dries, the marks vanish. Wet it and your route appears. Dry the map to make it disappear.

No escape?

This spy has been captured and stripped of his spy equipment. He can write one letter but it mustn't look at all suspicious. Luckily, his captors don't know that 'Mother' is the name of his spy chief. They've also left him all he needs to write an invisible letter. (See the next page to find out how he does it.)

Double meanings

Once he's written the letter, the spy must warn his chief that it contains an invisible message. He puts in special clues which have hidden meanings.

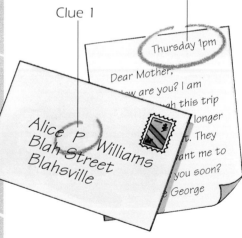

Clue 1

Clue 2

Thursday 1pm

Dear Mother,
...ow are you? I am
...h this trip
...longer
...t. They
...ant me to
...you soon?
...e George

Alice P Williams
Blah Street
Blahsville

Clue 1 is a false initial. The chief doesn't have a middle name. The false initial tells him there's an invisible note inside. The time in clue 2 tells him where the note is written. '1pm' means 'on the back of the letter.'

Invisible inks

The captured spy can write to his chief with either apple juice or wax. Whichever he chooses, he will leave clues in the letter, so the chief knows which one to look for.

As soon as he knows where the spy is being held, the chief can plan his escape.

1. Juice message

To write in juice, the spy sharpens one end of a matchstick, by rubbing it on the rough stone wall.

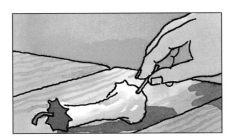

Then he pokes it into the fleshy part of the apple core to collect some juice, and writes with it.

If his chief heats the paper in a cool oven (300°F, 150°C, Gas Mark 2), the juice will 'cook' and darken.

2. Wax message

The spy can also use the candle. First, he breaks off some long, thin pieces of candle drips.

He warms the wax in his hands and rolls it into a pencil shape. He can write a note with this wax pencil.

To see the note, the chief sprinkles chalk dust over the paper and shakes it off. The dust sticks to the wax.

Testing for secret messages

Take care when testing for invisible messages. Start by holding the paper up to the light at an angle to check for tell-tale glints. Have your materials ready, so you can run through each test.

As well as chalk dust, you can use powdered coffee to look for wax. If your apple juice messages are faint, try using lemon juice instead.

Order of tests
1. Use powder to test for a wax message.
2. Use heat to test for a juice message.

Powder

11

Codes and secret messages

Despite your best efforts, sometimes the enemy will obtain your messages. If you want to be sure they won't be understood, you can write them in code. Use the initials of the code's name to tell your contact which code you have used, such as BR for 'Bi-Rev'. Each code below scrambles the phrase 'Spies on radio' in a different way.

Rev-Random

1. OIDAR NO SEIPS
2. OI DAR NO SEIPS

1. Write the message back to front.
2. Break the letters into new groups.

Bi-Rev

1. (SP)(IE)(S O)(N R)(AD)(IO)
2. (PS)(EI)(O S)(R N)(DA)(OI)

1. Break up the letters into pairs.
2. Write each pair back to front.

Mid-Dummy

1. SP IE SONRAD IO
2. S P IE SON RAD I O
3. SUP ICE SONDRAD IDO

1. Break the message into even-numbered groups.
2. Split each group in half.
3. Put a dummy letter in the middle of each group.

Rev-Groups

1. SPI ESON RA DIO
2. IPS NOSE AR OID

1. Form the letters into different groups.
2. Write each group back to front.

Sandwich

1. S P I E S O
2. SNPRIAEDSIOO
3. SNPRI AE DSIOO

1. Write out the first half of the message, leaving a space between each letter.
2. Write the second half in the spaces.
3. Group the letters differently.

Pendulum

1. SPIES   ONRA   DIO
2. _S_ _ _   _ O_ _   D_ _
3. _PS_ _   _NO_   _ID_
   PSI   _NOR_   IDO
   EPSI   ANOR

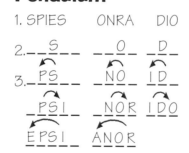

1. Re-group the letters.
2. Mark a space for each letter, putting the first letter of each group in the middle.
3. Add the rest from left to right as shown.

Keyword alphabet

In this code you exchange each of the letters in your message with the matching letter of a keyword alphabet.

Choose a word or short phrase (the keyword) in which no letter is used more than once. 'Careful Spy' is the keyword used in the example below.

Write it out beside the alphabet. When you have run out of letters in your phrase, continue with the rest of the alphabet.

Plain alphabet	Keyword alphabet
A	C
B	A
C	R
D	E
E	F
F	U
G	L
H	S
I	P
J	Y
K	B
L	D
M	G
N	H
O	I
P	J
Q	K
R	M
S	N
T	O
U	Q
V	T
W	V
X	W
Y	X
Z	Z

Newspaper messages

Make sure your contact gets the paper before the enemy.

Newspapers are useful for sending secret messages because they don't look suspicious. Leave the paper where it won't look out of place, such as on a park bench.

Crossword messages

Most magazines and newspapers have a crossword in them. Fill in the blank squares with a message. Only write going down. Fill the other squares with any letters. No one bothers to look at a finished crossword so make sure you fill in all the gaps.

Pin-hole messages

Find the date on the front page of the newspaper. Prick a hole with a pin over a number in the date. This tells your contact on which page to find the message.

Turn to that page. Prick holes over the letters to spell out your message. Prick a hole in the space between the printed words to show the end of a word.

To read the message, fold the paper so that the page with the message has no other pages behind it. Hold it up to the light. You will see the pin holes.

Tips for code breakers

To test your skills and keep in practice, try exchanging coded messages with friends. When decoding a message, write it in large capital letters, with plenty of space below each line. If the code has been made by exchanging one letter of the alphabet for another, remember the hints on the right.

1. Try to find vowels (AEIOU) and the letter Y. Every word has at least one of them.
2. Look for the one-letter words A and I.
3. Double letters are probably OO or EE.
4. A common pair of letters is TH. The most common three-letter word or part of a word is THE.
5. Don't rely on punctuation. It's probably false and put in just to fool you.

▷ Quick codes and broken codes

Using symbols is a good way to code a message quickly. Each symbol stands for a different letter of the alphabet.

Three symbol codes are given here. The different ways to write the word 'Danger', using each of the codes, are shown below.

Pig-pen code

Here, lines or a shape and a dot are used to represent each letter of the alphabet.

Semaphore

In this code, letters are shown like the hands of a clock.

Angle code

This code has a right angle and a number. Each angle is numbered from 1 to 7.

PLAIN	PIG-PEN	SEMAPHORE	ANGLE
A	⌐	①	1
B	⊔	①	2
C	∟	①	3
D	⊐	①	4
E	☐	①	5
F	⊏	①	6
G	⊏	①	7
H	⊓	①	1
I	⌐	①	2
J	·	①	3
K	·	①	4
L	·	①	5
M	·	①	6

PLAIN	PIG-PEN	SEMAPHORE	ANGLE
N	·	①	7
O	·	①	1
P	·	①	2
Q	·	①	3
R	·	⊖	4
S	∨	①	5
T	>	①	6
U	<	①	7
V	∧	①	1
W	∨̇	①	2
X	>̇	①	3
Y	<̇	①	4
Z	∧̇	①	5

Broken codes

To find out if the enemy has broken your code, write a message in it, saying future messages will be left at a new drop. Say where it is.

Write a message in a false code and hide it at the new drop. Warn your contacts not to collect it. Check to see if it is picked up.

If it is, your code has been broken. Change the codes and choose new drops at once. Leave only false messages at the old drops.

Morse Code

Sometimes, you won't be able to send written messages. Instead, use Morse Code to tap out a message. You can also use it to flash a message in the dark.

Good spies are inventive. If you don't have a flashlight, you could cover a lamp with your hat to flash a message.

Dots and dashes

Morse Code is made up of dots and dashes. It can be written out like this:

Your contact should write down each dot and dash as he receives them. He can then take his time decoding the message later.

Tapped messages

Tap on water pipes or radiators in a building. Make two quick taps for a dot and four for a dash.

Tap on walls with a pencil. Outside, you can tap on railings. Your contact will have to be close to them.

On soft ground, tap on a stone with a stick.

You can tap on the ground, too. Your contact must put his hand on a stick and his ear on that hand to hear.

Flashed messages

Switch the flashlight on and off.

Keep the flashlight on for a count of 'one' for a dot and 'two' for a dash.

In a room with a light on, draw the curtains and flap the edge of a curtain.

Pull the blind halfway down for a dot and close it for a dash.

If the room has a roller-blind, you could pull that up and down.

✏️ Emergency signals

You can also pass silent messages to contacts under the nose of the enemy, by doing something which seems innocent, but has a secret meaning.

At a meeting, for example, you could send a message by arranging your pens, pencils, eraser and ruler in a certain way, along the top of your desk.

Pencil code

Another silent message can be sent by putting a red, green and blue pencil in your top pocket, in a code order.

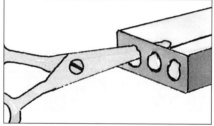

To make a pencil code set, first make three holes in the end of a matchbox tray, big enough for the pencils.

Put the pencils in the holes and wind a rubber band around the tray. Then push the tray into the box.

Face code

Danger!

Keep away!

Meet me later.

I've got a message.

Go to HQ.

Follow me outside.

This simple face code is probably the easiest of all to use in an emergency.

Sit with your first finger on, or pointing to, different parts of your face.

Each place you point to has a different meaning. Try not to look too obvious.

Secret code ring

With a code ring, you can communicate secretly with your contacts. See below for how to make one.

Different beads on the ring send messages without arousing the enemy's suspicions. Try to look casual when you change beads, or switch the ring between fingers.

Choose what kind of message each finger will give.

First finger could be used for emergency signals.

Middle finger could show times.

This finger could show places.

Little finger could show people's names.

Be sure to have a signal that means 'No message'.

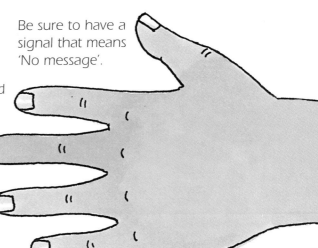

How to make a code ring

1.   2.   3.   4.

1. Cut a piece of fuse wire long enough to make a double ring around your middle finger.
2. Twist the two strands of wire tightly together.

3. Make four tubes of rolled up paper: one blue, one red, one yellow, one green.
4. Slip them over one end of the wire and join the ends of the ring.

Emergency	
	Follow me
	Danger
	Run
	Meet me later
	No message
	Our code's broken

Time	
	Today
	Tomorrow
	Morning
	Afternoon
	Midday
	Ten minutes

Write down what each combination of beads and fingers means in a code book. You could put the words in code in case the enemy finds your book.

Enemy alert!

Suppose you are waiting for a secret meeting with your contact when an enemy spy arrives.

To warn your contact not to give himself away, slip the code ring onto your finger.

Move your code ring to the bead meaning 'Danger!' Your contact will walk on, unsuspected by the enemy.

Disguise

To be sure spies aren't recognized when they're visiting a drop or out on a mission, they learn how to disguise themselves. Disguises let a spy keep a close watch on the enemy, without the risk of being discovered. When choosing a disguise, bear in mind the tips given here.

Wear clothes that help you to blend in with your surroundings.

When you are out on a spying mission, during the day or at night, act in a way that looks ordinary.

Remember: however good the disguise, if you draw attention to yourself, you may blow your cover.

Try to avoid being photographed. That way, the enemy has no record of your face.

Hide behind things wherever possible, trees, for example. This lets you keep an eye on suspicious-looking people without looking suspicious yourself.

Change disguises quickly to confuse the enemy. Change as often as you can.

If all else fails, use tricks to get away. Keep the enemy watching and waiting long after you've gone.

Quick cover ups

If it's sunny, hide behind a sunshade.

There are lots of tricks for keeping your face covered. An umbrella is useful for hiding behind.

Always carry a large handkerchief in your pocket. You can whip it out and use it in an emergency.

You could pretend to drop some money. But make sure that the enemy spy doesn't help you to pick it up.

If you are carrying a large bag or briefcase, you can bend over and pretend to look for something in it.

In a real emergency, the only way to keep your face hidden might be to tie your shoelace.

Always be prepared to take action. You never know where the next enemy spy may be lurking.

Another newspaper trick

Newspapers are vital pieces of equipment. Hidden behind a paper, you can watch two spies at once.

Make sure only your eyes peek over the top of the newspaper and that neither spy can see your face.

When both spies have passed, fold up your paper and follow them to their secret destination.

Disguise hints

Sometimes spies need a disguise that will let them stay around without looking out of place.

This is especially important if they are keeping watch on a building that is being guarded.

If, instead of just watching, they can pretend to be doing something else, they are less likely to be spotted.

Baffle enemy spies by wearing the same clothes as local people.

Bright lights

Keep in the shadows at night. Try to avoid the glare of street lights and lighted windows.

Familiar smells

Beware of dogs that know you. They will recognize you from your smell, no matter what your disguise.

Bluff

If you're on a mission with a friend, you can help them by causing a diversion which distracts the enemy.

Double bluff

For this trick, dress the same as a friend. Hide your faces as you pass the enemy spy.

Once you have gone, he is sure to follow, hoping to discover your HQ.

Now separate, and set off in opposite directions. He won't know who to follow.

All change!

Agent Z is an expert at quick-change disguises. You might pick up some ideas from the story of his latest mission. He was told to collect a file of secret plans from a luggage locker at the airport. But enemy spies had been tipped off and were keeping watch.

Z arrived at the airport in a taxi.

Wearing a suit, he looked like a businessman on his way to a foreign city.

He strolled to the toilet, completely unnoticed by the enemy spy.

With the coast clear, he quickly changed into a new disguise.

He reappeared in uniform, as a repair man working at the airport.

Pretending to repair a broken locker, he collected the file.

Then he returned to the toilet and put on his third disguise.

Finally, hiding behind a false moustache, he left.

Outside, he hailed a taxi to take him back to HQ.

The enemy was stumped – the file was gone.

People watching

If you are thinking about a new disguise, try watching other people to see how they behave, but do it carefully. Most people don't like being stared at, and some of them might be spies too.

When people sit down, some cross their legs. Others sit with their legs stretched out.

You can study how people carry things. Some are more used to doing it than others.

Look at people when they're asleep.

Watch people when they eat too.

Some open their mouths and snore. Others let their heads fall forward.

Everyone eats in a different way. Some eat carefully and slowly.

Others gobble their food and spill it.

Checking disguises

You may have a brilliant disguise – but so may the opposition. It is very important to recognize when other people are in disguise. Then you'll be prepared for any tricks they might play on you.

Offer to rub a smudge off someone's face, if you think they're disguised with make-up.

Wet hand shake

Carry a damp sponge in your pocket, to wipe your fingers on secretly.

When you shake hands with a spy wearing make-up, some may come off.

False beard trick

To get a closer look at a suspicious beard, pretend there's an insect in it.

Decoys

Spies use a decoy, or dummy, to fool the enemy into thinking they're in one place, when they're in another.

Spies often do their most secret work at night, but they never go out leaving their beds empty.

A spy away on a night mission will place a dummy under the sheets to trick an enemy spy.

Who's watching who?

This spy is trapped in his house. An enemy spy has stood outside, not moving, for five hours. But all is not as it seems.

Spy shadow

This trick shows you how to collect a secret document from your HQ and escape without being followed.

Enter the building and switch on the light. You want the enemy spy to see your shadow.

This is because it's not your shadow at all. Instead, it's a dummy sitting in front of the window.

The enemy spy will soon get tired of watching 'you' doing nothing. Now's your chance to slip away.

The enemy spy is just a decoy made up of a few wooden planks, shoes and a hat.

Change your looks

Using simple cosmetics can make a big difference to the way you look. You can buy cheap cosmetics in lots of stores.

Try out different techniques in front of a mirror. You will need cleansing cream and tissues to wipe the cosmetics off.

Choose cosmetics you can easily remove.

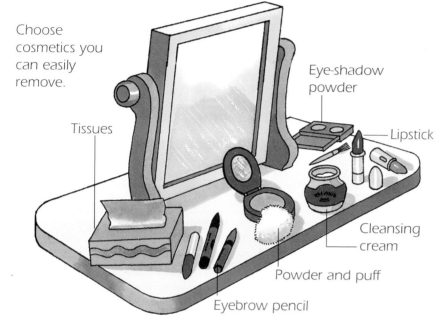

Tissues

Eye-shadow powder

Lipstick

Cleansing cream

Powder and puff

Eyebrow pencil

A black eye

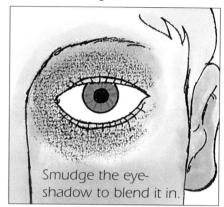

Smudge the eye-shadow to blend it in.

To pretend you have a black eye, brush blue eye-shadow around it.

Old eyes

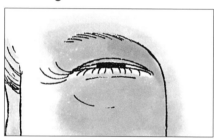

Crinkle up your eyes so you can see the wrinkles in the corners. See where the creases form.

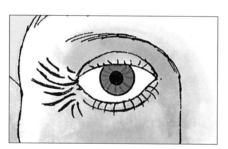

Draw thin, dark lines with a soft eyebrow pencil along each crease. This will make you look older.

Baggy eyes

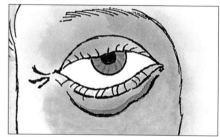

The skin under some people's eyes hangs down in 'bags'. Draw them in with an eyebrow pencil.

Eyebrows

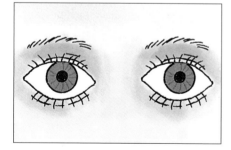

Altering your eyebrows can give you a totally new appearance.

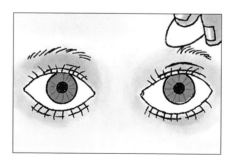

Rub on thick soap to blot out your eyebrows and wait for the soap to dry.

Use black or brown.

When your eyebrows have vanished, draw new ones with an eyebrow pencil.

Special effects: 1. A sling

A sling is very easy to slip on and off quickly. Take a scarf or piece of cloth and fold it in half.

Then hold it under your arm and put one end around your neck. Ask a friend to help you.

Lift the bottom end and tie it to the end around your neck. Use a loose knot that you can easily undo.

2. Cuts

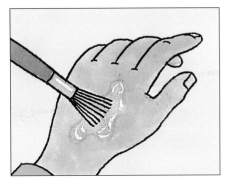

Smear some latex glue on your skin. As it dries, pinch the skin together, to make it look like a cut.

Using a washable felt tip pen, draw down the line of the cut. Make dark stitch marks along each side.

3. Missing teeth

You can buy special make-up, to paint out some of your teeth, from a party or costume store.

4. A head wound

A large bandage is a good way to disguise your hair.

Use a crepe bandage, or a long strip of white material. Begin with it rolled up and wind it around your head.

Bind it firmly, so that it won't slip when you're out. Fix the end with a safety pin, or tuck it in.

5. One-eyed spy

Cut out a piece of black cardboard. Put a hole in each of the top corners and thread black elastic through.

Looking older

You can make yourself look older by wearing clothes that are too big and not very bright. Choose clothes that look bulky and warm.

An 'old person' disguise is useful on a secret mission. Knitting gives you a good excuse to sit and watch what's going on.

Dark hats, glasses and a walking stick will help your disguise.

Old people are often a little unsteady, so move slowly. Hold onto the banister when going downstairs.

Sometimes, old people stoop. This makes them look shorter. They shuffle their feet and use walking sticks.

They are also stiff and bend down slowly to pick up something. It's a good way to sneak a look around.

Most old people look innocent. If you are disguised as an old person, you shouldn't be spotted.

You also have a reason to walk slowly and stop to rest. This is useful when collecting information.

If you pretend to be out shopping, you will be able to hide easily among a crowd of people.

Older faces

People's faces change as they grow older. If you look at old people, you will see lines around their eyes and mouths. Sometimes, they have hollow-looking cheeks too.

You can make yourself up to look older. Don't forget to change your hair to match. Old people often wear hats. A hat is a very good way to disguise your hair.

Lips

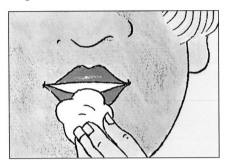

Rub pale foundation cream over your lips until they are the same shade as the rest of your face.

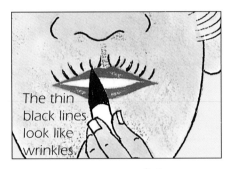

The thin black lines look like wrinkles.

Draw on a new, thin mouth with lipstick. Then draw thin lines around your mouth with a dark pencil.

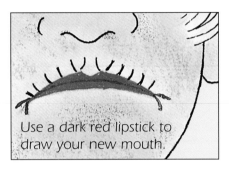

Use a dark red lipstick to draw your new mouth.

Now make a face, pulling your mouth down at the corners. Draw dark lines where you can see creases.

Shadows

Look at your face to see where the hollow parts are. Feel it with your fingers to find the main bones.

Try brushing dark blue eyeshadow around your eyes. Shade it at the sides of your face.

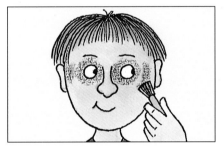

Put dark powder shadows in the hollows between the tops of your ears and your eyes.

Brush shadows on your cheeks below your cheek bones. This will make them look hollow.

Shadows on each side of your nose will make it look thin. Dab powder under your nose and mouth too.

Use a powder puff to dab pale face powder over the parts of your face where there are no shadows.

Improving your disguise

How you walk and stand can give you away, even if you are well disguised or the enemy is too far away to see your face. Try out the different walks shown here and match them to your disguises.

You could try walking quickly. Hold your head up and lean back. Keep your hands behind you.

Stiff leg

Pretend you have a stiff leg. A scarf tied around one knee makes it hard to bend.

Limp

Limp on one leg as if the other one hurts. Don't forget which leg it is.

Slouch

Take small steps and shuffle your feet. Put your hands in your pockets. Hunch over.

Bounce

Wear high-heeled shoes and take very small steps. Bounce as you walk.

Shuffle

Wear large flat shoes and shuffle along. Lean forward with your head down.

Stride

Walk quickly, with big strides, swinging your arms. Put your heels down first.

Toes in

Turn your toes in as you walk and lean forward a little.

Toes out

Turn your toes out and bend your knees. Put your feet down flat and stomp.

Bent back

Walk slowly.

Bend to one side, with your hand on that hip as if you have a bad back.

Change your shape

You can change your overall shape using padding. Put the padding on top of your normal clothes and wear bigger clothes on top of that. Don't forget to wear big shoes and gloves to complete the outfit.

A small towel around your shoulders will make them look broad.

Scarves around your arms and legs will fill out your clothes.

You can make your stomach look larger by tying cushions around your waist.

Beware of a bad disguise!

Nothing will blow your cover more quickly than a sloppy disguise or careless action. Some of these spies, disguised as waiters and guests, look very suspicious. How many suspicious-looking people can you see? (Check page 48 for the answer.)

Spy games

H ow good are your disguises? Play this game with several friends to find out. Arrange with them to be somewhere fairly crowded, at a certain time, and to stay for about fifteen minutes. Each of you then dresses up in your best disguise. No one should be able to recognize anyone else.

Make sure your disguise will fit in with where you're going. It could be a park – anywhere with people.

Go to the place at the right time. Move around, trying to spot the others, without being seen by them.

Think of a reason for being there. You could pretend to be shopping or delivering a package.

Carry a notebook and pencil with you. Write down the names of the friends you spot and the disguises they are wearing.

Also make a note of what the others are pretending to be doing. When the time is up, go home and take off your disguise.

Then meet to compare notes. Score a point for every disguise and action you guess right. The person with the most points wins.

Spying around the world

A spy may be sent on a secret mission anywhere in the world. He must wear the right clothes to fit in. This spy has dozens of hats. Which hat or head-dress will he need for each of the countries shown below?

A Scottish tartan cap

An American cowboy hat

A Swiss lace cap

An Arab head cloth

A Mexican straw hat

A Russian fur hat

1.

2.

3.

4.

5.

6.

Answers: 1. = a Russian fur hat   2. = a Scottish tartan cap   3. = a Mexican straw hat
4. = an Arab head cloth   5. = a Swiss lace cap   6. = an American cowboy hat

Shadowing

Secretly following a suspect is called shadowing. When you shadow someone, move quietly and try to stay hidden. Wear clothes that match your surroundings. This is called camouflage.

A camouflage headband

Cut a band of material long enough to go around your head and a piece of ribbon about 1m (3 feet) long.

Pin the ribbon to the band with safety pins, one at each end and four or five more in between them.

Choose twigs, leaves and grass to match your surroundings. Push them between the pins like this.

Clothes should be old and tough for crawling in, but smooth enough not to catch in spiky bushes.

How to shadow

Walk silently and smoothly, trying not to move too quickly. Swivel your eyes to look around you, rather than moving your head.

Don't stand or walk on the skyline – everyone will see you.

Keep shiny things out of the glare of the sun.

When you stop, stay in the shade. Make sure your shadow doesn't give you away.

On the scent

If the suspect has a dog, you must stay downwind of it. Otherwise the dog may sniff out your scent.

To check the wind's direction, wet a finger and hold it up. The colder side of your finger faces upwind.

You can also toss a handful of grass or dry leaves into the air. They will blow downwind.

Walks and crawls

Keep your head down.

Things that hide you are called 'cover'. Where there is good cover, like trees, you can walk upright.

Near low cover, like a wall, you may have to crouch. Hold your thighs to keep you in the crouch position.

Holding your thighs also helps you to keep your balance. Don't shuffle. Lift your feet off the ground.

Cat crawl

Crawl on your hands and knees, keeping your back flat and low.

Lift your feet just clear of the ground. Try not to bob your head.

Flat cat crawl

The inside of your knee should touch the ground.

Lie slightly on one side, with one leg straight and the other bent.

Press on your forearms and bent knee to raise your body and push it forward.

Seal crawl

Start flat on your tummy with your legs together and your toes turned out.

Reach out, pull with your forearms and push with your toes to move forward.

Using cover

Think carefully about how to use the cover around you. The spy in the black hat, above, can be seen very easily.

You only need one eye when looking around a wall or tree. This makes your head less obvious.

Shadowing in town

In town, there is less cover. A spy must follow his suspect closely enough not to lose her, but not so closely she grows suspicious. He can glance at her, but he mustn't stare. He could pretend to look around, as if looking for a friend.

Using your eyes

One useful trick is to move your eyes from right . . .

. . . to left, without moving your head.

Stop!

Never stop and start when your suspect does. He'll notice. If you must stop, have a good reason.

You could:
* buy a newspaper
* look in a store window
* pretend to be waiting to cross the road.

Corners

Be careful as your suspect nears a corner. If you're not looking, he may be out of sight before you realize.

Go after him, but slow down before the corner. Walk around it casually. He may be bluffing too.

Window check

If you can see your suspect's reflection, he can see yours.

How can you tell if your suspect is watching you in the reflection of a window?

Move so that you are behind him and he cannot see your reflection.

If he is keeping an eye on you, he'll move to try and catch sight of you again.

Trick of the trade

Pause in a doorway to change.

When you are shadowing, try to carry a quick disguise kit. You can change into it if you are spotted.

Take something different from your first outfit. Carry it in a bag which you can hide in your pocket later.

Behind you!

You can use a spyscope to spy over your shoulder. (See the box on the right for how to make one.)

The spyscope is a mirror which is disguised to look like a diary. You could hide a mirror in a comic book.

Make a spyscope

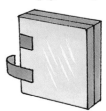

Fasten tape here.

Tape two handbag mirrors shiny sides together. Make sure you can open and close them easily.

Glue one page to each side of the spyscope.

Tear all but the first and last pages out of an old diary. Slip the mirrors between them to make the spyscope.

Shaking off a shadow

It's important to remember that an enemy spy might try to shadow you too.

To avoid being followed or 'tailed', use the tips in the picture below.

Follow the spy in the brown hat and see how he shakes off the enemy spies.

Use reflections in store or car windows to see if you are being followed.

Enemy spies are in blue coats.

Look for side streets. Slip down them when your enemy's view is blocked.

When crossing a street, wait until you are shielded by other people.

Spy's view blocked by van.

Shadowing practice

Successful shadowing takes a lot of practice. Try these games with your friends. They train you to listen for the tiniest sound, to move silently or to stay still in one place.

Searchlight game

You play this game outside. One of you is the guard, who is blindfolded and carries a flashlight. The rest are prisoners. They must creep from the start to the guard without being seen.

The guard calls, "Ready!" and the prisoners set off. If the guard hears a noise, he points to where he thinks the prisoner is and shouts, "Freeze!" Then he turns on the flashlight and looks over his blindfold.

Prisoners

Use stones to mark the start.

Guard

The guard stands in front of a second row of stones. The first prisoner to reach them wins.

The winner becomes the next guard.

True "Freeze!"

FREEZE!

If a prisoner is caught in the flashlight, he must go back ten paces. Everyone else stays still. When the flashlight is switched off, the game continues.

False "Freeze!"

FREEZE!

If no one's there, the guard has called "Freeze!" unfairly. If he does it three times, he loses the game. The prisoner nearest him becomes guard.

Beat the guards

Two players, in blindfolds, stand on either side of an open door. One by one, the others creep from the wall opposite, through the door. If a guard hears a player, he puts out his arm. If the player is touched, he goes back to the wall. A player who gets past becomes a guard.

A training course

Use a training course to teach you to move silently. One of you is the trainer. Stand with your back to the course. One by one, the others try to touch you. Each time you hear a noise, call out. The player you heard loses a point. See who loses the least points.

Take turns being the trainer.

Planks on bricks

Try to walk on the planks without rattling the stones.

Crawl under the lids without clanging them.

Tie a string between two sticks. Hang 'clanging lids' from it, fairly low down. See the box below for how to make clanging lids.

Arrange some cans so you have to move carefully to go past them. Stack them or put in stones which will rattle if you touch them.

Cover parts of the course with things that crunch or rustle when you step on them. Try gravel, twigs, dry leaves or newspaper.

Clanging lids

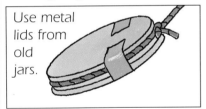

Use metal lids from old jars.

Tie a piece of string around each lid. Knot it and hold it in place with strips of tape.

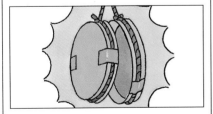

Hang the lids on the string close together. Then they will clatter if one of them is touched.

Hide and shadow

READY!

This is an outside game for two. Choose a tree trunk or large stone as your 'base'. One of you waits here while the other hides.

The aim of the game is to find the other player before he finds you. Both players can move around once the game has started.

Tracking a suspect

Until a spy becomes an expert at shadowing, he may lose sight of his suspect. If that happens, he will need to look for clues to see where she has gone. The clues might be easy to spot, like footprints, or less obvious, like a broken twig. Following clues like this is called tracking.

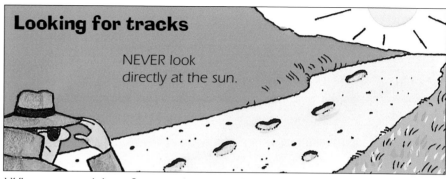

Looking for tracks

NEVER look directly at the sun.

When searching for tracks, shield your eyes and look in the direction of the sun.

If there is even a small dent in the ground, it will cast a shadow.

Covering your tracks

Be careful that you don't leave a trail for a spy to follow. Try to walk on hard or stony ground, short grass or fallen leaves. Here are some extra tips for confusing your tracker in the countryside.

Look ahead and plan your route across safe ground, like the carpet of dead leaves in these woods.

Step on ferns or big leaves to avoid making footprints in mud or sand. Pick up the leaves as you go.

Don't walk on the soft edges of roads and try to avoid sandy paths.

Use stepping stones to cross a stream. Don't get wet feet or you'll leave damp footprints.

If you have to cross a patch of mud, walk facing away from the direction you're going.

If you leave footprints, make sure they won't give you away. A tracker might recognize them if you have holes in the soles of your shoes.

Using landmarks

Sometimes, you will come to places you don't know. If that happens, look out for things you will remember to help you find your way back. These are called landmarks. In towns, you can use churches or stores. In the country, you could use farmhouses or gates. Here are some more ideas for things to look for.

Warning!

Only choose objects that can't move. Try to look back from time to time too, because things can look very different when you're going the opposite way.

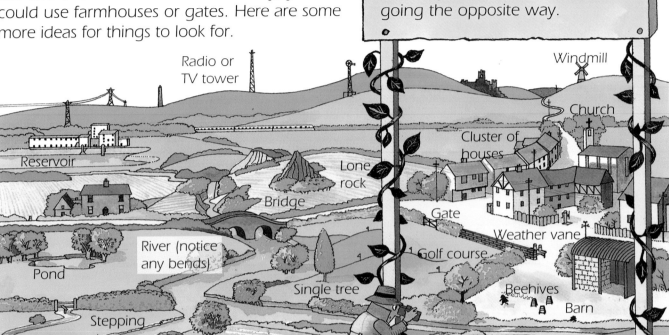

Radio or TV tower
Windmill
Church
Cluster of houses
Reservoir
Lone rock
Bridge
Gate
Weather vane
River (notice any bends)
Golf course
Pond
Single tree
Beehives
Barn
Stepping stones
Scarecrow

A tracking stick

A tracking stick is a useful gadget which can help you improve your tracking skills. You use it like a walking stick to leave a track for friends to follow.

Use the stick on soft wet ground or wet sand.

To make a tracking stick, you will need:
a metal lid with a rim, for example, from an old mayonnaise jar
a pair of pliers
a nail and a hammer
a thick walking stick or an old broom handle
a screw about 3 cm (1¼ inches) long
a screwdriver

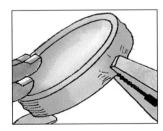

1. Make a kink in the lid with the pliers. This will show the direction you're going in.

2. Hammer the nail into the lid to make a hole. Then use the nail to make a hole in the stick.

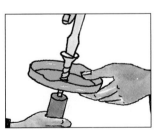

3. Ask someone to hold the stick steady. Put the lid on top of the stick and screw it on.

🪧 On the trail

When tracking a suspect, you might want to leave a trail for a contact to follow. Below are some signs you can use.

Make them with twigs, stones or deep scratches in the ground. They should be just large enough for your contact to spot.

Put them in sheltered places or they may be disturbed by walkers. Make sure that no one sees you laying the trail.

Go straight ahead

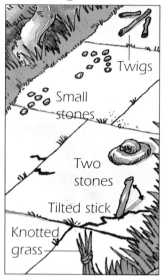

Twigs
Small stones
Two stones
Tilted stick
Knotted grass

Don't go this way!

Broken twigs
Row of stones
Crossed twigs

Caution!

Proceed with care: the enemy may be near.

Message hidden

The numbers show how many steps to go to find the message.

Gone home (end of trail)

Gone to hideout

Turn left
(Put the sign the opposite way to show turn right.)

Broken twig
Tilted stick

Picture signs

Here are signs for leaving more detailed messages. They are based on the picture-writing of the native American Sioux tribe.

The Sioux scratched their messages on dried animal skins and bark. You could use chalk on dry stones or a stick on the ground.

Time of day

morning

noon

evening

day

night

Weather and landscape

grass

road

rain

sun

lake

river

sea

tree

forest

Camp

hideout (camp)

camp fire

rations

meeting

hidden or hide

leader

discovery

many

Trail tips

A good trail layer only leaves signs where they are really needed. Use them to show a change of direction or where there is a choice of paths.

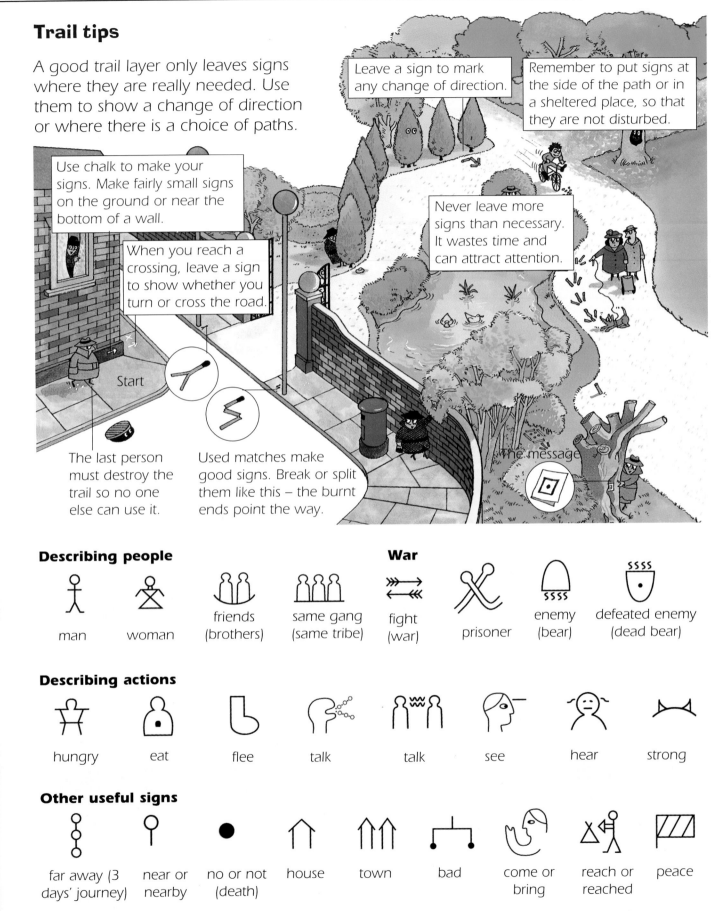

Leave a sign to mark any change of direction.

Remember to put signs at the side of the path or in a sheltered place, so that they are not disturbed.

Use chalk to make your signs. Make fairly small signs on the ground or near the bottom of a wall.

When you reach a crossing, leave a sign to show whether you turn or cross the road.

Never leave more signs than necessary. It wastes time and can attract attention.

Start

The message

The last person must destroy the trail so no one else can use it.

Used matches make good signs. Break or split them like this – the burnt ends point the way.

Describing people

man   woman   friends (brothers)   same gang (same tribe)

War

fight (war)   prisoner   enemy (bear)   defeated enemy (dead bear)

Describing actions

hungry   eat   flee   talk   talk   see   hear   strong

Other useful signs

far away (3 days' journey)   near or nearby   no or not (death)   house   town   bad   come or bring   reach or reached   peace

🐾 Track and trail puzzles

This puzzle tests how well you know the trail signs from the previous pages. Follow the signs on the ground in the picture below. Each time you come to a 'message hidden' sign, you'll see a clue for where to go next. The trail starts in front of the school. If you get stuck, the answer is on page 48.

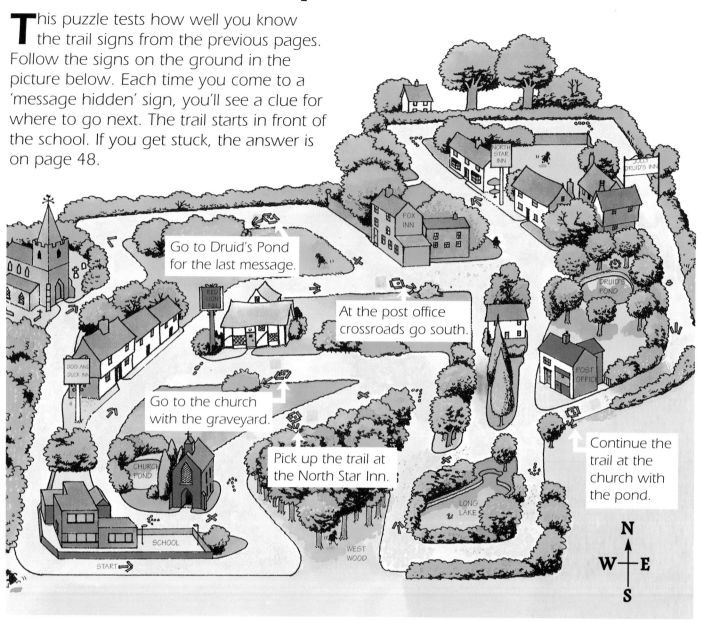

Go to Druid's Pond for the last message.

At the post office crossroads go south.

Go to the church with the graveyard.

Pick up the trail at the North Star Inn.

Continue the trail at the church with the pond.

N W E S

START →

Tracker's guide

A good tracker learns to recognize all the footprints, paw prints and tracks he sees.

It's always useful to know if a suspect has a dog with her or is using a stick.

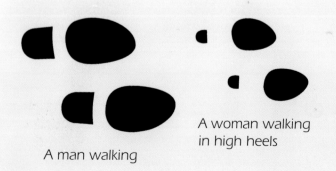

A man walking

A woman walking in high heels

A flat-footed man with a stick

A woman walking with a dog

Picture messages

Can you decode these picture messages? They're written in the Sioux signs from pages 40 and 41. Don't try to 'read' the signs one by one, like words in a sentence. Use your imagination to fill in the gaps. (See page 48 for the answers.)

1.
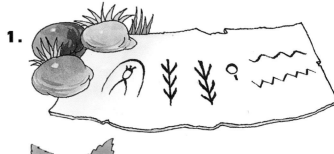

2.
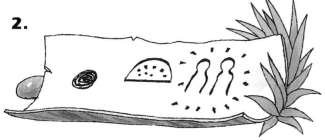

3.

4.

5.
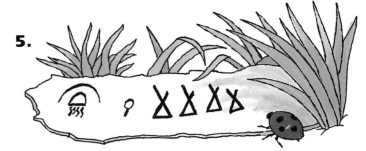

6.

7.
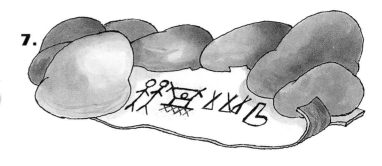

The best time to look for footprints is when there is snow on the ground.

You can also look on damp sand and patches of mud.

Dog prints

Cat prints

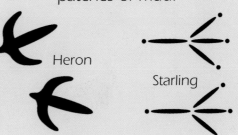

Heron

Starling

Following bird prints is good tracking practice.

Swan

Spy kit

To be well prepared on a mission, you will need to take some things with you. But only take the essentials. Everything should fit into your pockets. Your basic spy equipment can fit into a large matchbox.

The spy kit below holds your invisible writing kit (a candle for wax writing and chalk for wax developing), a hollow twig disguise, string and chalk for signpost signals and a mini-pencil for messages.

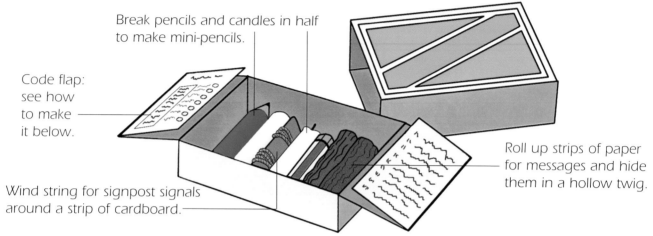

Break pencils and candles in half to make mini-pencils.

Code flap: see how to make it below.

Wind string for signpost signals around a strip of cardboard.

Roll up strips of paper for messages and hide them in a hollow twig.

Code flaps

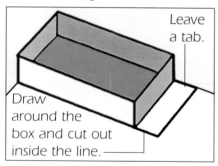

Leave a tab.

Draw around the box and cut out inside the line.

Cut two strips of cardboard, slightly longer and thinner than the box. Use the extra length to make a tab.

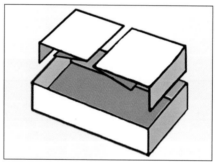

Fold the tabs down. Trim them to fit the ends of the box. Fold the strips so the flaps fit together in the box.

Write the codes on one flap and the meanings on the other. Then glue the tabs into the box.

Disguising the box

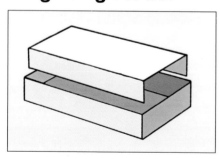

Cut a piece of cardboard a little shorter and wider than the box. Fold the ends so that it fits inside the box.

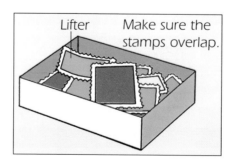

Lifter   Make sure the stamps overlap.

Glue some stamps to the cardboard. Leave part of a stamp unstuck. You can use it to lift the cardboard up.

Extra kit

Carry some nuts and raisins in a plastic bag.

Other useful things to take are a notebook, a map, a flashlight, and a snack in case you get hungry.

Quick disguise collection

You'll need lots of different disguises for your various missions. Ask your family and friends for old clothes they don't want anymore. Collect as many clothes, hats, shoes and bags as you can. Put long clothes on hangers, so they don't get wrinkled.

Hats —
Ties —
Boots —

— Gloves, belts and scarves
— Sunglasses
— Cheap rings and necklaces
— Bags and cases

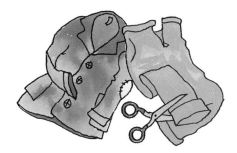

Cut off the ends of sleeves if they're too long. Snip around them as neatly as you can.

Stuff paper or pieces of rolled-up cloth into the toes of boots and shoes that are too big.

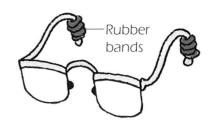

Rubber bands

Ask an adult to take the glass out of some old glasses. Put rubber bands on the ends to keep them from slipping.

Before setting out

Cut out the labels from clothes and shoes.

Before a mission, check your bags and pockets. Take out anything which might give you away.

You could make up an old diary with false names and places.

Write fake letters addressed to your false name.

Take things in a wallet to prove you're who you say you are, such as fake family photographs and letters.

Make sure that anything else you carry, such as pens or handkerchiefs, has your false initials.

Ready for a mission

By now, you should be ready for your first mission. Try these final tests to check your powers of decoding and observation. The answers are on page 48.

The codes used below are the quick codes 'Rev-Random', 'Bi-Rev', 'Rev-Groups' and 'Sandwich' from page 12. **HOT TIP!**

Where's the traitor?

These four spies are part of an international spy ring. Their code names are BAT, ELK, FOX and OWL. They have just found out that FOX is a traitor. Can you decode their conversations and then say which city FOX is in?

1. Paris calling Delhi

WONKU OY ODTA HW?

2. Delhi calling Paris

OF IX NS TO NI AC RI O

3. Delhi calling Cairo

RA YE UO LE K?

4. Cairo calling Delhi

ON ON TABR

5. Cairo calling Paris

EHW IER XOFS?

6. Paris calling Cairo

KLE ROT ABOT KLAT

7. Cairo calling Helsinki

IKLE ONS NIT RAP SI EHW IER TABS?

8. Helsinki calling Cairo

BNAD TEIL SHI I

Who stole the secret plans?

One of these spies stole secret plans from a top security office. Five people saw him leave. An old man thought his coat was brown.

A policeman said he wore dark glasses and had three buttons on his coat. An old lady said he was bald and had a briefcase.

A boy said he was wearing a spotted blue tie. The old man was mistaken, but the others were right. Which picture shows the spy?

1.  **2.**  **3.**  **4.**  **5.**

6.  **7.**  **8.**  **9.**  **10.**

 ## Spy language

Camouflage: clothes worn by a spy which blend into the background
Code-breaking: deciding which code a message has been written in
Contact: a member of your spy ring
Cover: anything a spy uses to hide behind, bushes or buildings for example
Drop: a place where messages are left by spies for other spies
Encode: putting a message into code

False drop: somewhere you pretend to leave messages, or leave messages written in a false code
Headquarters (HQ): the place from which a spy ring operates
Keyword: a word used to make a code
Master spy: the head of a spy ring
Rendezvous: a meeting between two spies
Shadowing: following and watching a suspect without him knowing

Signpost: the place a sign is left to show which drop is being used
Spy ring: a group of spies who work together secretly
Suspect: a person believed to be a spy or a member of an enemy spy ring
Tail: a spy who shadows another spy
Tracking: following the tracks, clues or footprints left behind by someone
Trail: the tracks left behind by a suspect, or clues left by a contact for a spy to follow

47

Answers to the puzzles

Beware of a bad disguise! page 29

Suspicious people have been marked with a star.

Trail puzzle page 42

1. By the school, follow the arrows to message 1 and the North Star Inn.
2. From there, follow the signs past the Jolly Druid's Inn to message 2 and the church with the pond.
3. Outside the church, follow the arrows to message 3, which sends you to the post office crossroads.
4. At the crossroads, follow the signs to message 4. This takes you to the church with the graveyard.
5. Follow the signs to message 5 and the final sign at Druid's Pond: 'Gone home'.

Picture messages page 43

1. Hide in the forest near the river
2. No night meeting
3. Bring rations to the camp fire in the evening
4. Meeting in the morning by the lake
5. The enemy is hidden near the camp
6. The leader of the enemy talks peace
7. People have discovered our hideout – flee!

Where's the traitor? page 46

Paris = Rev-Random
Delhi = Bi-Rev
Cairo = Rev-Groups
Helsinki = Sandwich

FOX is in Paris.
OWL is in Cairo.
BAT is in Delhi.
ELK is in Helsinki.

Decoded, the messages say:
1. What do you know?
2. Fox is not in Cairo.
3. Are you ELK?
4. No, nor BAT.
5. Where is FOX?
6. Talk to BAT or ELK.
7. ELK is not in Paris. Where is BAT?
8. BAT is in Delhi.

Here's how you solve the puzzle: You're told FOX isn't in Cairo. Then you learn that the spy in Cairo isn't ELK or BAT. He must be OWL. You know BAT is in Delhi. ELK isn't in Paris and he can't be in Cairo or Delhi, which leaves Helsinki. So FOX must be in Paris.

Who stole the secret plans? page 47

The spy who stole the plans is number 9. He is in dark glasses and has three buttons on his coat. He is also bald, carries a briefcase and has a spotted blue tie. His coat is yellow, not brown as the old man thought.

First published in 1999 by Usborne Publishing Ltd, Usborne House, 83-85 Saffron Hill, London EC1N 8RT, England. www.usborne.com
Copyright © 1999, 1990, 1978 Usborne Publishing Ltd.
The name Usborne and the device are Trade Marks of Usborne Publishing Ltd.